Steve Parish
PUBLISHING

HOW TO
DRAW Australian
Sealife

TEXT & ILLUSTRATIONS
BY KERRY KITZELMAN

Anemonefish

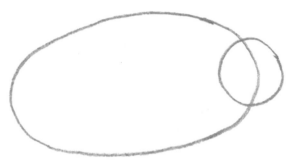

An anemonefish is also known as a clownfish. It lives among the tentacles of sea anemones, where it is protected from predators. An anemone's tentacles are lined with stinging cells that paralyse most small fish that touch them but, amazingly, not the anemonefish! This brightly coloured little fish can dart in and out of the anemone's tentacles without fear, protected by a special slime covering its body.

STEP 1.

Begin your masterpiece by drawing a large oval shape for the body and a small circle for the head. The two shapes overlap, with the oval passing through the centre of the smaller circle.

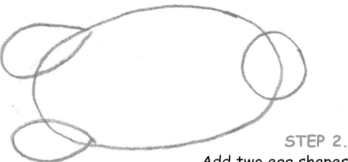

STEP 2.

Add two egg shapes as shown. These will be the rear fins.

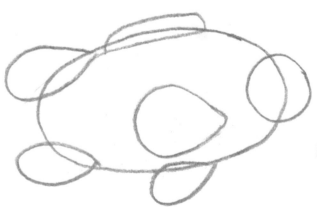

STEP 3.

A rectangular shape and two more egg shapes are drawn where the upper (dorsal) and lower (pectoral) fins join the body.

STEP 4.

Place the eye carefully and sketch in the position of the nose using a ">" shape.

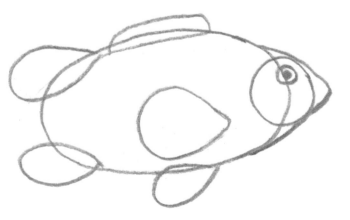

STEP 5.
Now it's time to position the tail using another circle a small distance behind the body of the fish. Join the tail to the body with curved lines.

STEP 6.
Carefully draw the pattern of colours you see on the anemonefish and then, using a black felt-tip pen or dark pencil, go over the outline.

STEP 7.
Complete all the details of the lips, fins and markings in black ink as shown. When finished, erase the pencil guidelines or paint over them.

Some anemonefish are called clownfish because of their bright colours. They often use their colours, and darting actions, to frighten away other fish that might want to eat the anemone.

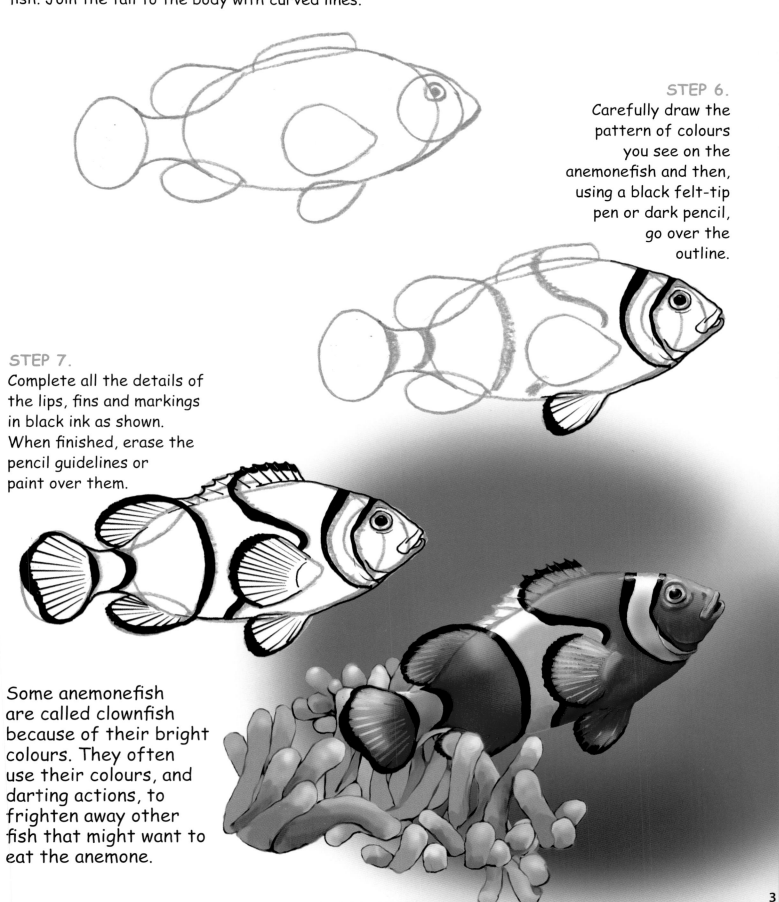

Australian fur-seal

Choosing only the finest seafood, an Australian fur-seal dines on fish, rock lobsters, squid and octopus. Although ungainly on land, in the water a fur-seal is graceful and swift. Its streamlined body slips effortlessly through the water as it chases food or plays with friends.

STEP 1.
Begin by drawing two egg shapes with the narrow ends facing outwards. The egg shape of the body is larger and stretched while the head is smaller.

STEP 2.
Draw another three elongated egg shapes, in varying sizes, to represent the flippers. The fourth flipper is hidden on the other side of the body.

STEP 3.
Using smooth lines, join the head to the body. Add a triangle to the front flipper.

STEP 4.
Let's also draw the rock the fur-seal is sitting on. (Drawing a seal is very easy, don't you think?)

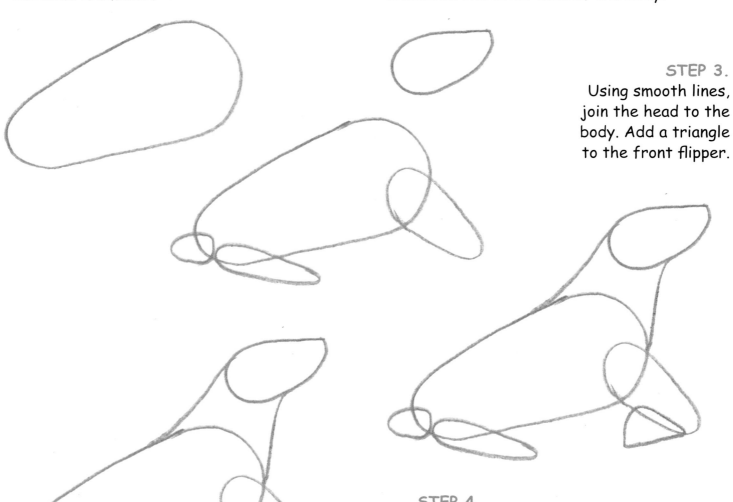

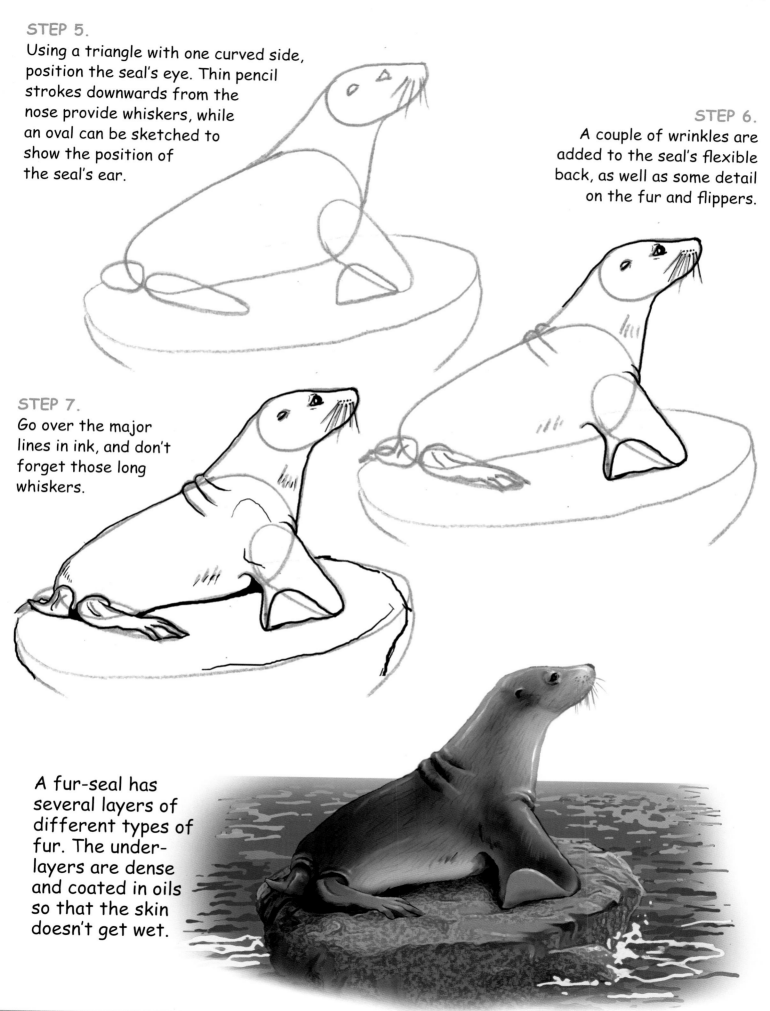

STEP 5.
Using a triangle with one curved side, position the seal's eye. Thin pencil strokes downwards from the nose provide whiskers, while an oval can be sketched to show the position of the seal's ear.

STEP 6.
A couple of wrinkles are added to the seal's flexible back, as well as some detail on the fur and flippers.

STEP 7.
Go over the major lines in ink, and don't forget those long whiskers.

A fur-seal has several layers of different types of fur. The underlayers are dense and coated in oils so that the skin doesn't get wet.

Billfish

A billfish is also called a swordfish, and for a very good reason. It uses its long, sharp snout to "stab" its prey. Broadbill swordfish have even been known to put holes in boats! When chasing food, an excited billfish may change the colour along its back and maintain a bright blue glow.

STEP 1.
Draw a large upside down teardrop for the body of the billfish and a straight line for its pointy bill.

STEP 2.
Add another smaller teardrop shape facing in the opposite direction to the first. Extend the line of the bill into a curve that runs along the body.

STEP 3.
To add the streamlined tail, position three triangles of different lengths and shapes at the base of the drawing. Take care to get their positions right.

STEP 4.
Detail can be provided to the head by drawing two thicker, slightly curved lines from the body to the bill. Draw in the mouth and large gills by using simple curves and straight lines.

STEP 5.
Use two narrow, curved triangles for the two pointed side fins. Using a wave-like curve, draw the dorsal fin along the back of the billfish. Note the position of the eye. A rectangle and triangle combine to make the bottom ventral fin.

STEP 6.
Once all the fins and other body parts are in place, draw over the main lines in black ink.

STEP 7.
Shade in the large fins on each side of the body. When complete, erase all of the guidelines.

A billfish is very fast. It can reach speeds of 100km/hr. When travelling at these speeds, it sometimes leaps clear of the water!

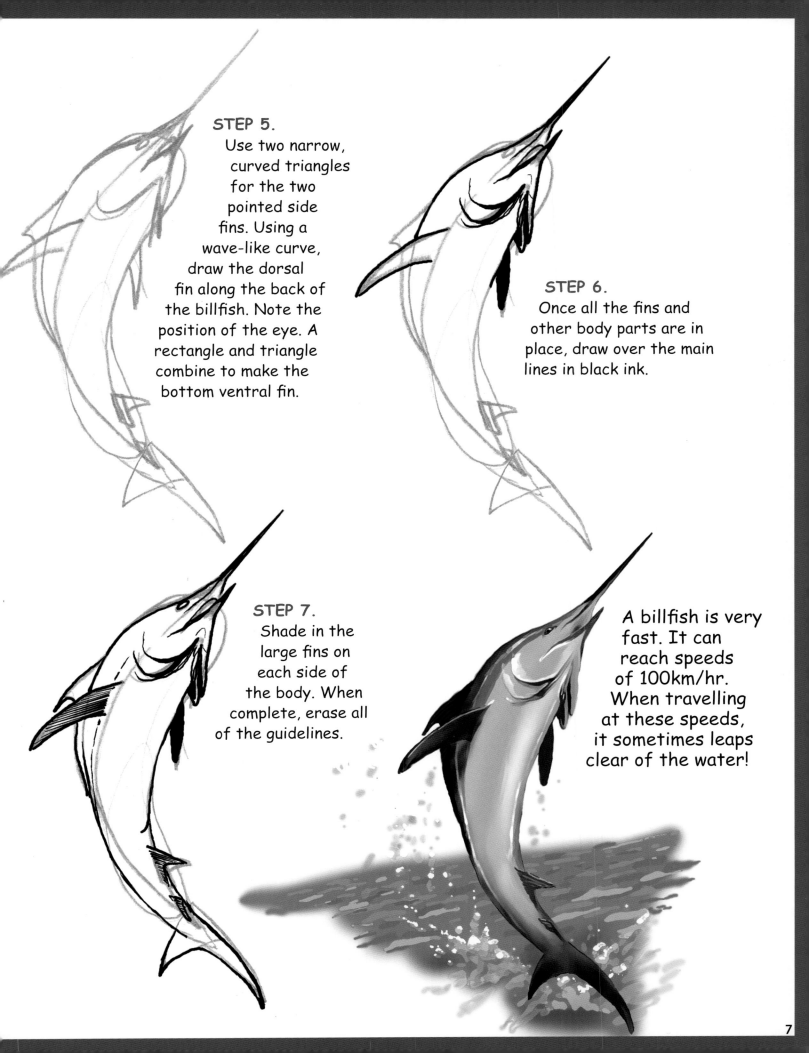

Dolphin

A dolphin is not actually a fish. It is a mammal that lives in a group called a pod and, unlike a fish, must come to the surface to breathe. A dolphin's body is sleek and streamlined. Propelled by a strong, muscular tail, it slips through the water at great speed chasing schools of fish.

STEP 1.

Dolphins have a rounded section of their head called a melon. So draw a small circle for the melon-head and a teardrop shape for the body.

STEP 2.

A smaller teardrop is used for the large muscles powering the tail, which is represented here by two small triangles.

STEP 3.

Triangles are the perfect shape for drawing the rest of the fins. Even the rostrum, the part of the dolphin's head that contains its mouth and jaws, can be added using a triangle.

STEP 4.

Using the shapes you have drawn as a guide, use smooth lines to sketch the outline of the body. Notice that the bottom jaw in the rostrum is slightly longer than the top.

STEP 5.
Use a small almond shape to mark in the dolphin's eye and the "blow hole" on top of its head. Add short, thin lines along the body to add detail and show the muscles in action.

STEP 6.
Begin going over the main lines in ink, starting with the outline. Take care not to make the shape of the fins too sharp.

STEP 7.
As the pectoral fin on the far side of the body will be in shadow, use shading to colour it in.

A dolphin uses echolocation to identify objects in front of it. Special sound waves produced by its melon hit an item and echo back, enabling objects to be located even before they can be seen.

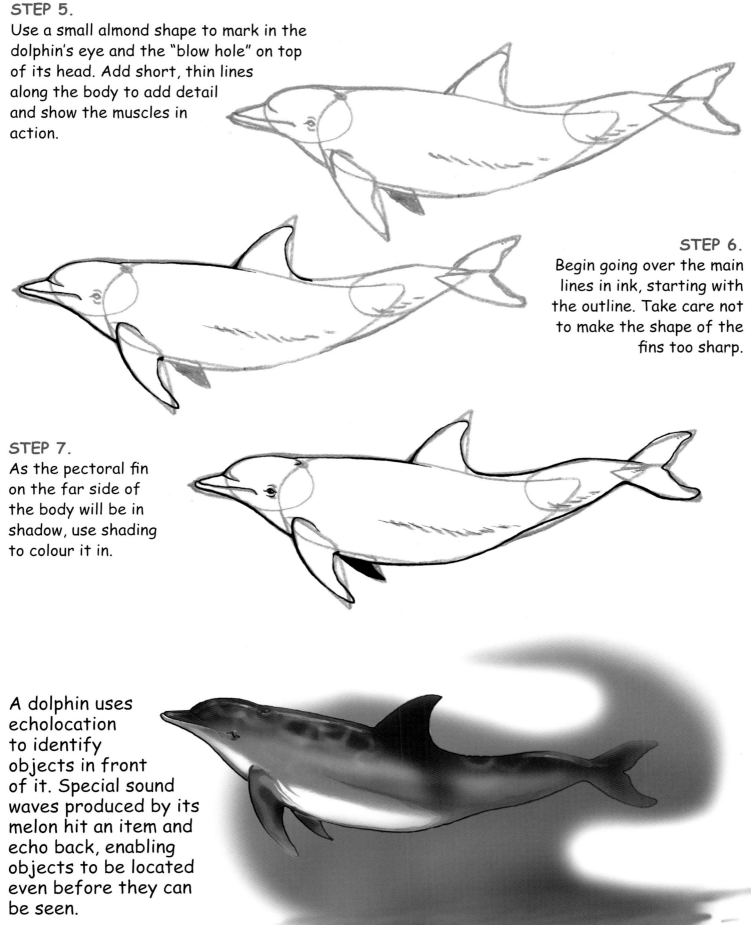

Butterflyfish

The long-nosed butterflyfish uses its elongated snout to probe coral crevices in search of shrimps. Side-on, this fish appears broad and brightly coloured. As it turns, its thin body makes it very difficult to see from behind. Predators become confused when they see a large, bright fish disappear in a flash!

STEP 1.

This is a very easy fish to draw. Start with a square and a triangle. These are the body and tail respectively.

STEP 2.

Add another triangle for the head, two circles for the eyes and a skinny triangle for the long snout. A second, smaller triangle here creates the lip.

STEP 3.

Draw a half circle, or arc, from one side of the square to the other to create the top, or dorsal, fin. A smaller half circle can be drawn on the underside for the ventral fin.

STEP 4.

Sketch the other fins as narrow triangles. Can you see the butterflyfish taking shape?

STEP 5.

Give the tail a fan shape and use two curved lines to suggest the shape of the body where it joins with the tail, then draw spines in the fins.

STEP 6.

After marking two curved lines for the gill flaps, shade part of the head to show the colour pattern of the fish.

STEP 7.

Use black ink to draw the permanent outline and to colour the dark parts of the fish's colour pattern.

The dark spot near the butterflyfish's tail also confuses predators because it looks like an eye. The real eye is hidden by the black pattern covering the fish's head.

Coral cod

A coral cod has a huge, wide mouth. It is an ambush predator that will hide in wait among coral and rock crevices. When unwary prey swims close, the cod rushes out at great speed, opens its enormous mouth and swallows the unsuspecting victim whole. The rapid opening of the cod's jaws sucks the prey inside.

STEP 1.

We will be drawing the cod facing us, so its head will appear rounder than its body. Use a circle for the head and a slightly thinner, but taller oval for the body.

STEP 2.

Draw two triangles pointing at each other to form the rest of the body and the tail.

STEP 3.

Use triangles, circles, arches, curves and zig-zags to sketch the rough shape of the fins. Be as accurate as you can.

STEP 4.

Inside the circle for the head, draw two oval shapes – one smaller than the other. Note their position relative to the head. These ovals will become the massive lips of the cod's mouth.

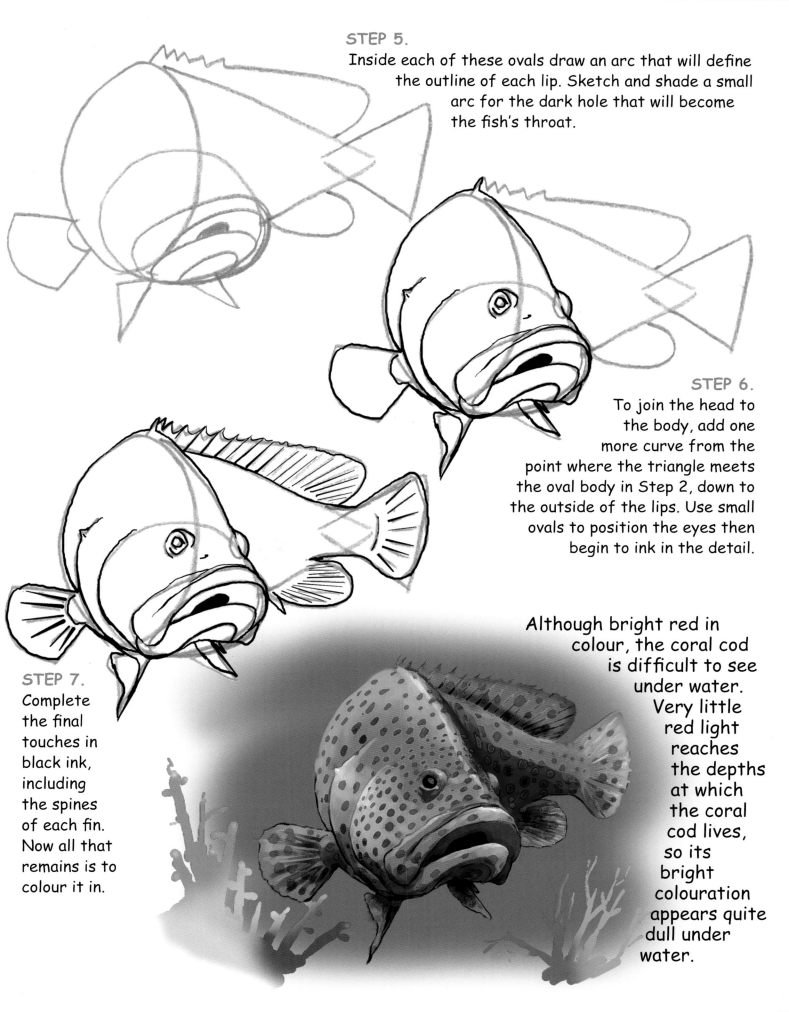

STEP 5.
Inside each of these ovals draw an arc that will define the outline of each lip. Sketch and shade a small arc for the dark hole that will become the fish's throat.

STEP 6.
To join the head to the body, add one more curve from the point where the triangle meets the oval body in Step 2, down to the outside of the lips. Use small ovals to position the eyes then begin to ink in the detail.

STEP 7.
Complete the final touches in black ink, including the spines of each fin. Now all that remains is to colour it in.

Although bright red in colour, the coral cod is difficult to see under water. Very little red light reaches the depths at which the coral cod lives, so its bright colouration appears quite dull under water.

13

Dugong

The dugong is a marine mammal that lives in warm, sheltered coastal waters. It spends most of the day grazing on meadows of seagrass, so it is sometimes referred to as a sea cow. A dugong may live for 70 years, grow to 3 m in length and weigh 400 kg!

STEP 1.
Begin with a circle for the head and a large fat oval for the body.

STEP 2.
The dugong has a most unusual snout with a large fleshy mouth. Draw another circle slightly smaller than the head – this will be part of the snout. Next, draw an egg shape under the circle you just completed, which will be the fleshy mouth used for grazing.

STEP 3.
An upside down teardrop and two triangles form the downward-facing tail.

STEP 4.
When a dugong feeds, it almost walks along the bottom of the sea with its front flippers. Two rectangular shapes are all you need to draw for the flippers.

STEP 5.
Complete the outline of the body and sketch in the horseshoe-shaped mouth and nostril. Position the eye in the bottom of the circle for the head.

STEP 6.
Use short, thin pencil strokes to add some whiskers around the snout. Begin going over the main guidelines in ink, adding shading where needed.

STEP 7.
Dugongs occasionally get struck by boats during their lives, leaving scars from propellers, so add three pencil lines on the back.

A female dugong only gives birth to a single calf once every 3–7 years. This extremely low rate of reproduction, combined with the disappearance of their seagrass meadows, places pressure on the survival of the dugong.

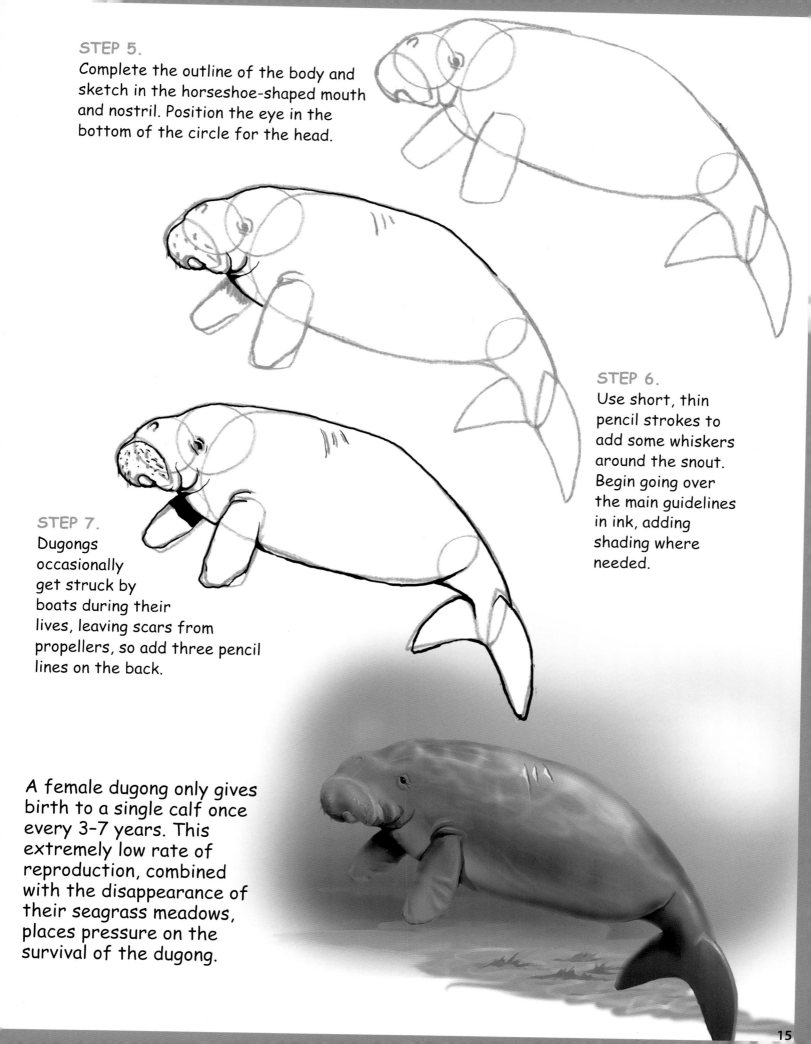

Emperor angelfish

Many scientists think that the intricate patterns of the angelfish break up its outline and confuse predators. This camouflage helps the angelfish merge with the patterns of the underwater reef in which it lives. Angelfish don't usually swim into open water. Most prefer to stay close to the protection of their reef home.

STEP 1.
Begin with a box shape for the angelfish's body.

STEP 2.
Add a couple of triangles for the head and tail.

STEP 3.
Add some more, narrower triangles for the fins. Note the slender shape of the fin close to the tail. Two small triangles joined at one side form the shape of a fin near the gills.

STEP 4.
Place the eye slightly above the centre of the triangle for the head and, using curved lines, begin sketching the pattern on the angelfish's body.

STEP 5.
Go over the outline of the box shape, rounding the corners and putting in some detail for the fins.

STEP 6.
Now you will need to take care as you draw the intricate patterns along the angelfish's body. Take your time and use graceful, flowing lines.

STEP 7.
Use black felt-tip pen to draw over the main lines and shade in the dark parts of the angelfish's body.

It's amazing that anyone could not see such a beautifully coloured fish. But in an environment filled with bright colours, that's exactly what happens!

Fiddler crab

Australian fiddler crabs make good neighbours! Scientists recently found that a male fiddler crab will help defend its neighbour's burrow from attack. A male fiddler crab has one enlarged claw, which he uses to wave at females to attract them. Females have two small front claws, used for feeding. Males with the biggest claw attract the most females.

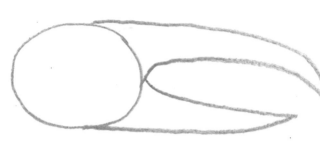

STEP 1.

Let's draw a male fiddler crab and start with its very large claw. Use a circle for the muscle of the claw and two curved triangular shapes for the pincers.

STEP 2.

Now sketch two small, overlapping circles behind the claw. These two small circles are the segments of the claw's arm. The arm joins the claw to the body of the crab which is drawn as a large flattened oval in the background.

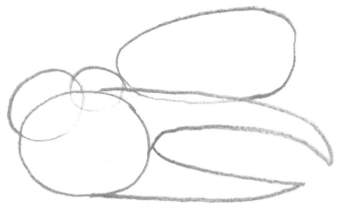

STEP 3.

Two more ovals look a little like eyes in the crab's body. The crab's real eyes are on stalks represented by two thin rectangles, each with a small oval drawn on top.

STEP 4.

On the right side of the body, start sketching the legs of the crab using a rectangle, two ovals and pointed triangles for the other, smaller claw.

STEP 5.
Use a rectangle for the segments in each of the legs. It can get very confusing when you are drawing several legs, so it is recommended that you only draw two, then use a felt-tip pen to ink in their outlines before drawing the segments for the other legs.

STEP 6.
Using black ink, go over the outline completed so far. Then you can continue drawing in rectangles for the remaining leg segments.

STEP 7.
Once all of the legs are drawn, finish the drawing using black felt-tip pen.

Males only have one small claw, which is used for feeding, so they spend twice as much time feeding as females do.

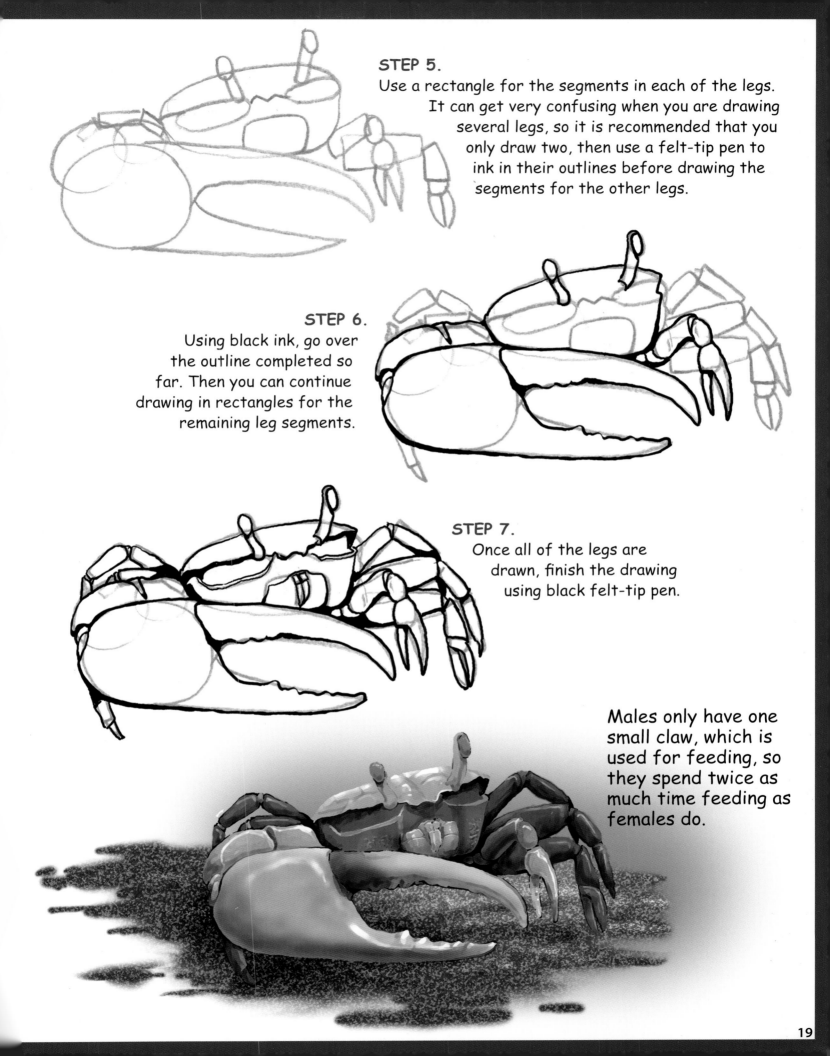

Green turtle

Although swift and graceful in the water, a green turtle is very heavy and ungainly on land. In the water, the front flippers do all the work while the hind flippers are mainly used for steering. Most sea turtles only visit land to lay their eggs and then retreat to the ocean.

STEP 1.
Use a thin egg shape for the turtle's shell and a circle for its head. Turtles can pull their heads in, but this one will have its head out, so place the head a little way from the body.

STEP 2.
Sketch the front flipper as shown and join the head to the shell with a long neck.

STEP 3.
Draw a circle where the front flipper meets the shell. Also draw the rectangular hind flipper and triangular tail.

STEP 4.
Draw another large oval shape covering most of the top half of the shell. In this oval we will draw the scales that make the shell. Like all reptiles, the turtle is covered in scales. Some of the scales fuse together to form the shell. Use a curved line from the front flipper to the back to show the edge of the shell. This is where the top half of the shell joins to the bottom half.

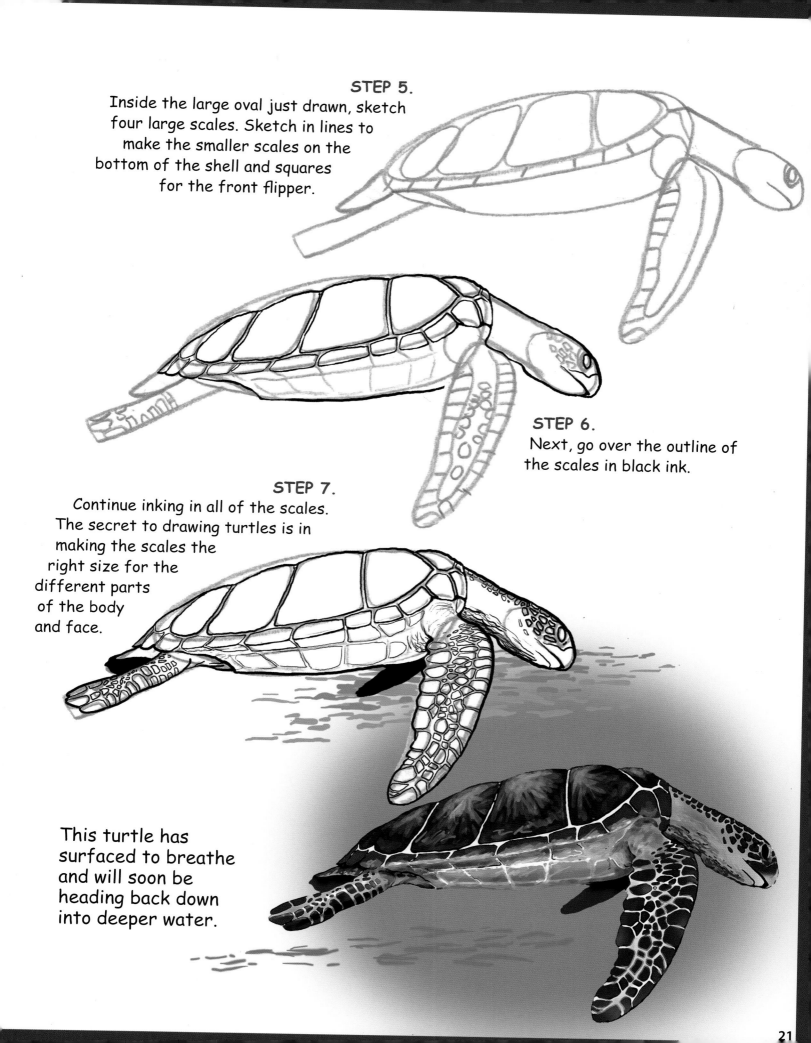

STEP 5.
Inside the large oval just drawn, sketch four large scales. Sketch in lines to make the smaller scales on the bottom of the shell and squares for the front flipper.

STEP 6.
Next, go over the outline of the scales in black ink.

STEP 7.
Continue inking in all of the scales. The secret to drawing turtles is in making the scales the right size for the different parts of the body and face.

This turtle has surfaced to breathe and will soon be heading back down into deeper water.

Humpback whale

Bigger than a bus, a humpback whale is an awesome sight when it frolics in shallow waters close to shore. Whales were once almost hunted to extinction, but since hunting has been stopped in Australia their numbers are slowly increasing. In winter, they travel northwards to warm, coastal Australian waters to breed, returning to Antarctica in summer.

STEP 1.
Two long teardrop shapes are drawn for the head and body, as shown.

STEP 2.
Draw a crescent moon shape for the whale's tail.

STEP 3.
Now add the large, oval pectoral flipper (called a fluke) and a small, triangular dorsal fin.

STEP 4.
Next, sketch the mouth using a squiggly line like the one drawn here. Put the eye inside the oval of the head – close to the bottom of the head but just above the line for the mouth.

STEP 5.

Let's put a few barnacles on the lower jaw and draw some of the grooves that can usually be seen on the belly of humpbacks. Complete the outline, joining the head to the body.

STEP 6.

The front edge of a humpback's fluke is often bumpy. After drawing in the bumps, start using black ink to go over the outline and main lines.

STEP 7.

Use ink to sketch the details around the eyes, mouth and jaws.

A humpback whale will often slap the water surface with its tail or fluke to attract the attention of other whales.

Octopus

An octopus has a soft body and eight long tentacles. Each tentacle is covered in many suction cups to grip onto rocky ledges and hold on to prey, such as crabs. If in danger, some octopuses will squirt ink into the water and disappear behind the purple or black haze.

STEP 1.
Begin by drawing two circles for the head and body.

STEP 2.
Draw another two circles, one inside the other, for the eye of the octopus. Two triangles joined together form the web of skin where the tentacles join onto the body.

STEP 3.
Now it's time to sketch in the tentacles. Note that each tentacle is thickest where it joins on to the body and thinnest at its end.

STEP 4.
Most often the ends of the tentacles curl up like tendrils.

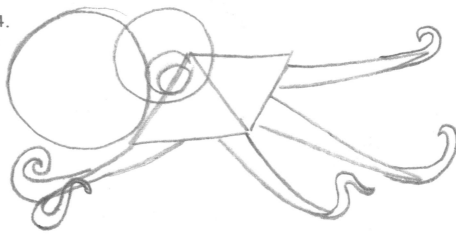

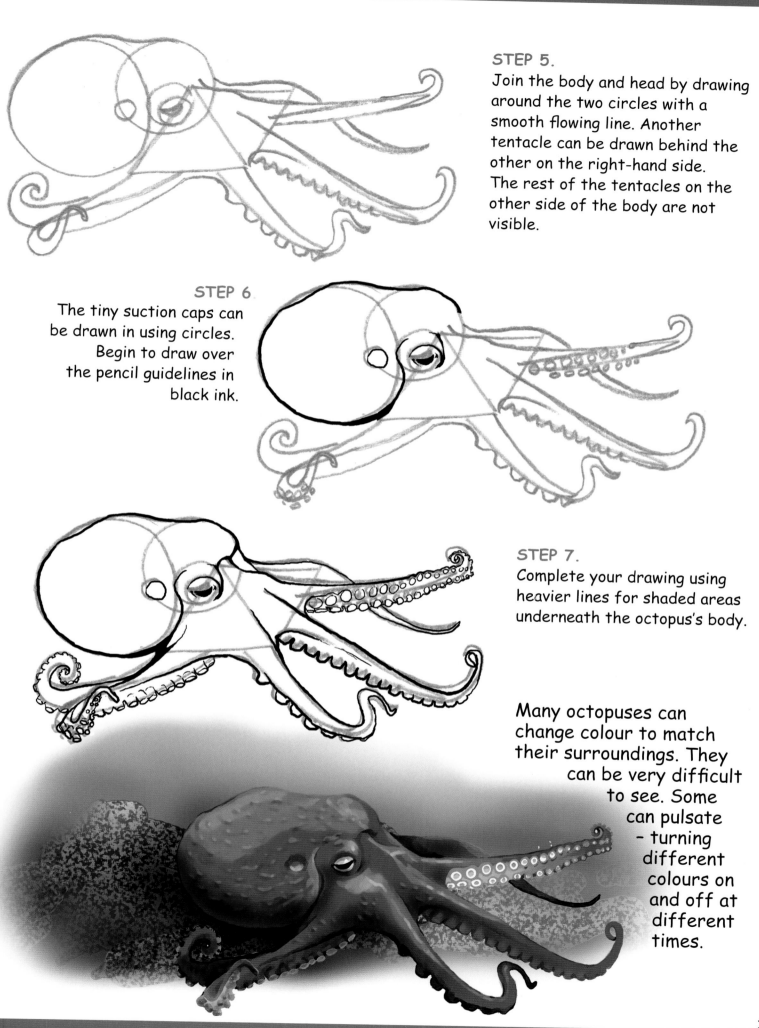

STEP 5.

Join the body and head by drawing around the two circles with a smooth flowing line. Another tentacle can be drawn behind the other on the right-hand side. The rest of the tentacles on the other side of the body are not visible.

STEP 6.

The tiny suction caps can be drawn in using circles. Begin to draw over the pencil guidelines in black ink.

STEP 7.

Complete your drawing using heavier lines for shaded areas underneath the octopus's body.

Many octopuses can change colour to match their surroundings. They can be very difficult to see. Some can pulsate – turning different colours on and off at different times.

Seahorse

Life for a young seahorse can be very uncertain. Only two out of every thousand survive to adulthood – most fall prey to crabs and fish. The curly tail of the seahorse helps it to grip tightly onto weeds and corals in the hope of blending in and hiding from predators.

STEP 1.
Draw a small oval for the head and a larger, egg-shaped body.

STEP 2.
A long graceful neck is drawn using a curved line that continues down the back and forms a curly tail.

STEP 3.
Sketch in the other side of the tail and neck as shown.

STEP 4.
Draw a thin rectangle for the long snout. The smaller rectangle at the end of the snout will become the seahorse's mouth.

STEP 5. Draw an eye by placing a small circle inside another just above the nose. Use small arches to create bumps along the back and a rectangular bump on the head. Draw the small dorsal fin on the back using a wavy line.

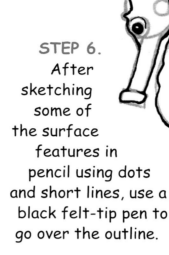

STEP 6. After sketching some of the surface features in pencil using dots and short lines, use a black felt-tip pen to go over the outline.

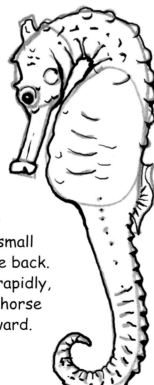

STEP 7. Complete the drawing by adding internal details. Don't forget the small dorsal fin on the back. This fin, beaten rapidly, moves the seahorse forward.

The large bump on the head of a seahorse is called a coronet. Just like a fingerprint, the coronet of every seahorse is different.

Shark

Cruising through the water, sharks are always on the lookout for their next meal. A shark's skeleton is made from cartilage, making it very flexible and relatively lightweight. A shark is perfectly suited to a predatory life in the sea. Sharks have several rows of teeth. As the teeth in the first row wear down or break off they are replaced by those behind.

STEP 1.

Begin with an oval for the shark's sleek body. You can make the shark fat or thin depending on the shape you draw.

STEP 2.

Using triangles, add a dorsal fin to the top and a pectoral fin to the side near the bottom of the oval.

STEP 3.

Two pointed triangles form the nose and mouth of the shark.

STEP 4.

Sketch two sloping lines at the back of the body. Additional triangles can be placed on these lines for the second dorsal fin, pelvic and anal fins.

STEP 5.

Now draw two more triangles, as shown, to form the general shape of the tail. (It's starting to look like a shark already!)

STEP 6.

Sketch the details of the head, teeth and gills in pencil. With a black felt-tip pen, go over the main lines you've just drawn.

STEP 7.

Continue to ink in the main features as you work towards the tail.

Most sharks have to keep swimming to stay afloat, but the grey nurse shark comes to the surface to swallow air which it holds in its gut to help with buoyancy.

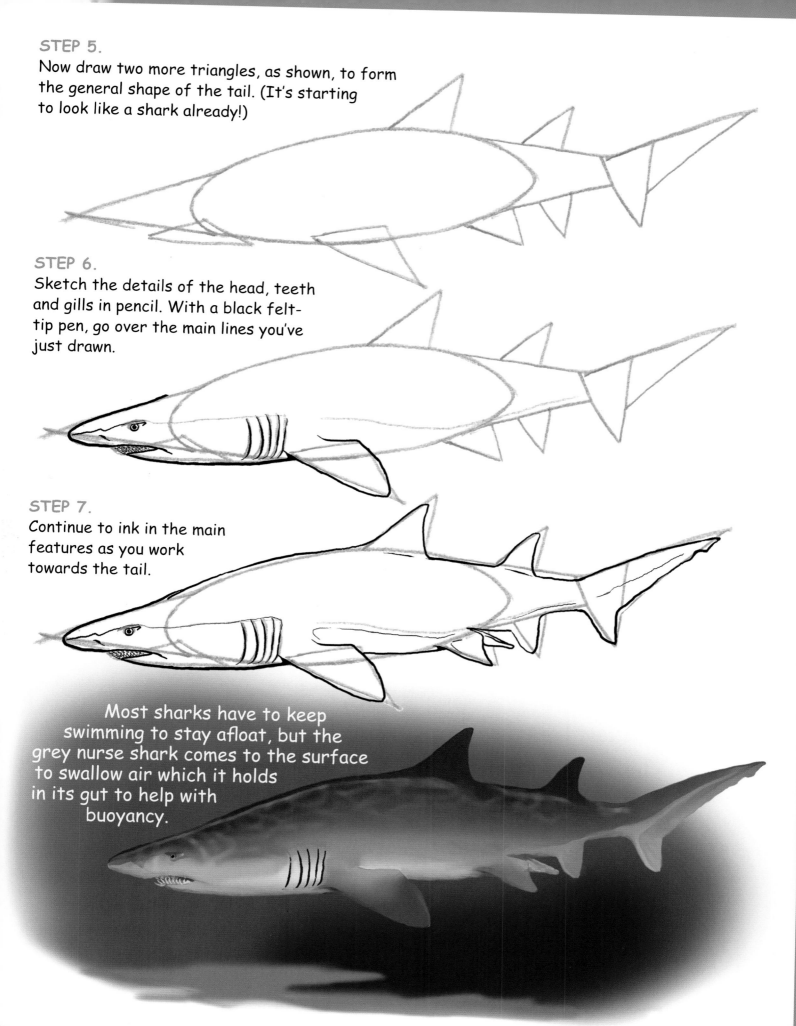

Stingray

The skeleton of a stingray is also made from cartilage. A stingray's flat, disc-like body usually hugs the sea floor, and sometimes a stingray will cover its body with sand, leaving just its eyes visible. Many stingrays have a spine or sting in their tail, which produces venom in a gland near its base. A sting from a stingray spine can be very painful.

STEP 1.
Stingrays are shaped like a huge fried egg. So let's draw a similar shape to start with.

STEP 2.
Two teardrop shapes are sketched in to mark the position of the eyes.

STEP 3.
A long straight tail stretches out behind and can be drawn using two slightly curved lines.

STEP 4.
Stingrays move by rippling their bodies in a smooth, wave-like motion. Draw a couple of wavy lines along one side of the body.

STEP 5.
Draw a similar wave-like line on the opposite side, but don't add too many waves or it may look unnatural.

STEP 6.
Now go over the outline with ink. Draw double lines on parts of the stingray's flaps to indicate the thickness of their edges.

STEP 7.
Use a sharp triangle to draw the sting, which is hidden in a sheath of skin. Complete the stingray by adding lines around the eyes, back and head.

A stingray may be adorned with beautiful patterns, which may help camouflage the stingray so that it is able to hide from predators.

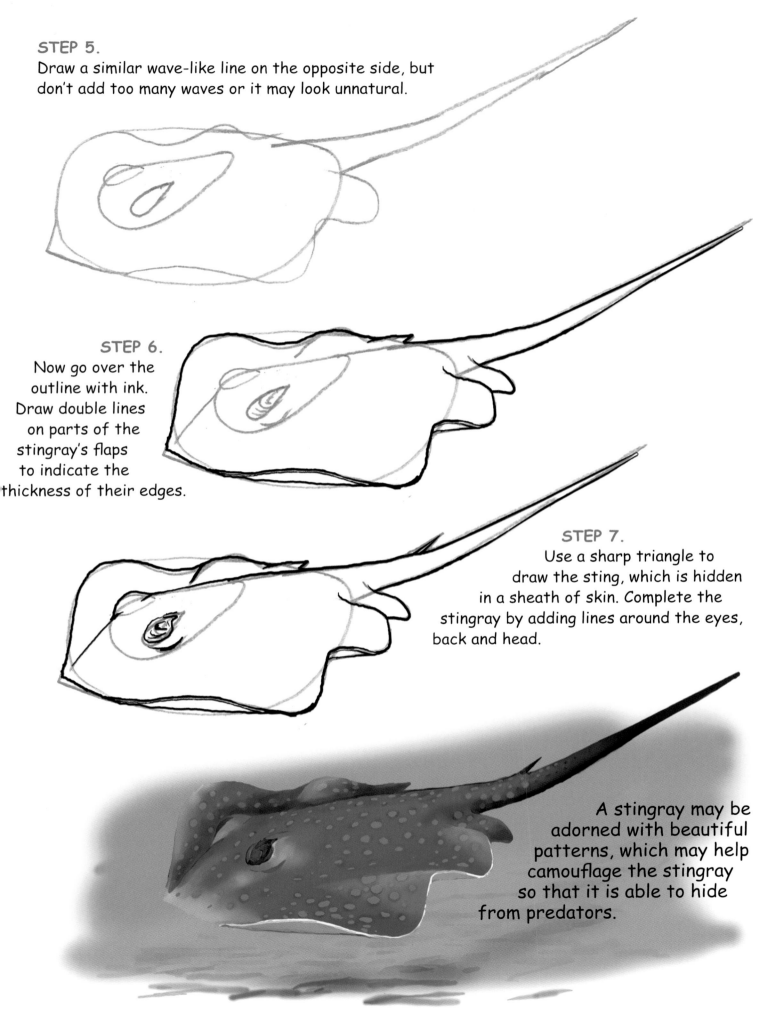

The Finishing Touch

While the focus of this book is on how to draw sealife, each illustration is finished in full colour.

Before adding colour you must choose your "medium", which is what you will use to add the colour. The choice is immense. You may already have coloured pencils, felt pens and crayons. More recently, computer technology has expanded your options even further. If you choose to use paints, such as acrylics or water colours, here's a few tips to keep in mind.

Just like when you draw, when painting careful observation of your subject is essential to getting the right "look". Colours in nature often change with the light. Late afternoon light tends to bathe everything in warm yellows and reds, while in the middle of the day the colours are often more vibrant and true.

Distant objects may appear more blue than red. A distant red object usually seems maroon or purple rather than true red. Even white objects in the distance appear to be pale blue. Closer objects are brighter in colour. Therefore, when applying colours, objects in the background should not be as vivid as those in the foreground.

To add shadow, use blues and browns, but keep the time of day in mind - use blue shadowing for midday and brown for the afternoon. Smooth rounded surfaces have soft shadows that are blended gradually, but hard, sharp edges have high-contrast shadows with crisp edges that require very little blending.

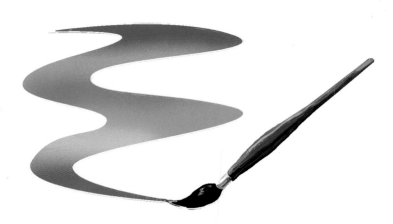

Finally, don't be afraid to experiment. The good thing about making a mistake with paint is that you can always paint over it!